Beginners Guide to Circular Knitting Pattern

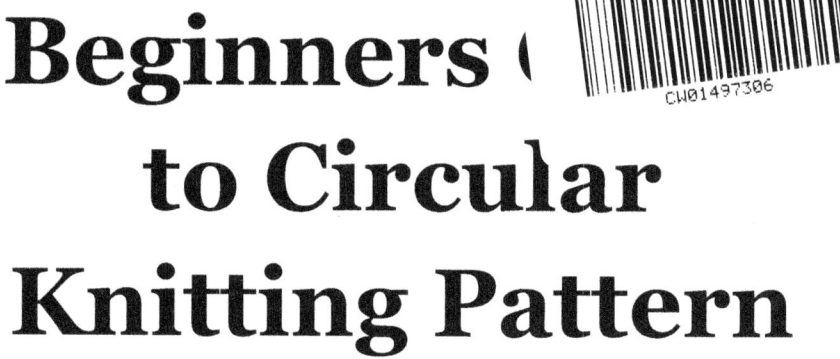

Mastering the Basic DIY Patterns
and Projects for Newbies

Jane Blinks

Table of Content

Introduction

A circular knitting machine, or a circular knitter, is a type of knitting machinery widely used in the textile industry to produce various types of knitted fabrics, garments, and accessories. These machines are designed to create seamless knitted products known for their comfort, flexibility, and durability. The circular knitting process involves using multiple needles arranged in a circular configuration, which work together to create knitted fabric in a continuous loop.

The concept of circular knitting machines can be traced back to the early 19th century, with the invention of the first circular knitting frame by William Cotton in 1804. However, it was not until the late 19th and early 20th centuries that significant advancements were made in the design and functionality of these machines. In 1874, William Cotton's son, James Cotton, patented an improved version of the circular knitting frame, which led to the widespread adoption of circular knitting machines in the textile industry.

In this research, we compiled instructions and examined the advantages and disadvantages of various types of knitting machines.

Circular knitting machines are very flexible to create fine, attractive, and complex patterns without stress. Circular knitting machines are a famous puck for individuals wanting to begin their knitting journey and looking to create a complex, attractive, fine design without stress. For beginners, knowing the foundation of the machines and the art of circular knitting is very important. The machines enable stress-free knitting in the round, making the hem look perfect, also ma and

For individuals who are just starting with circular knitting machines, there are some designs that they can start with without any stress. One of the most common designs is the basic ribbed pattern, which can be done using various types, colors, and textures of yarn.

Another one that can be used for starters is the simple stockinette stitch cowl, which is very good for releasing tension and learning to stitch well. After one has learned the foundation and basic designs, one can move to complex patterns like lace or cable knit patterns.

Another crucial area that should be considered when a beginner is picking the right yarn and the needle size for the project. Various types of yarn weights and needle sizes will give different results, so checking, experimenting, and seeing what works best for you is crucial.

Another important thing needed in making a good design on a circular knitting machine is knowing how to read and follow the design instructions and getting familiar with the common knitting techniques and terms so that the individual can confidently do any project that comes their way.

Circular knitting machine designs for individuals are just starting to have a very rewarding and fun way to check through different machines and make fine, attractive handmade items. Practice makes perfect. With practice and patience, get a machine and some materials, and then be ready to go on the creative journey in the world of circular knitting

Chapter one

Fisherman Scalloped Baby Blanker

The fisherman scalloped baby blanket knitting machine is a good, efficient, and flexible tool that has been used for a long time. It is used to make nice, attractive, and complex baby blankets. The machine is very simple, and it has nice, effective designs. It enables the knitter to make scalloped edged easily, makes knitting easier and more enjoyable for the person knitting of all skill levels, and makes the blanket look elegant and nice.

One main characteristic of the fisherman scalloped baby blanket knitting machine is its capacity to make scalloped edges on a finished blanket. This makes the blanket look decorative and enhances its overall appearance.

Also, the machine has features like adjustable settings that enable people to navigate their knitting projects according to their liking. The machine can take all it needs if they want it to be tighter or looser.

Using the fisherman-scalloped baby blanket knitting machine is easy, straightforward, and enjoyable. By taking some simple steps, the knitter can make nice blankets that will be treasured by the parents or loved ones.

The type and quality of the blankets made from these machines cannot be unmatched, as every stitch is being slowly crafted with care and precision. The result will be a soft and cozy blanket that will help keep babies comfortable and warm for many years.

In summary, the fisherman scalloped baby blanket knitting machine is a timeless tool anyone can use and cherish. It is enjoyed worldwide and can be used to make knitting enjoyable and create a beautiful, high-quality baby blanket with ease and very beautiful.

Instructions

The fisherman scalloped baby blanket knitting machine is a flexible and very easy-to-use machine that can be used to make fine and beautiful blankets for little ones. Following the instructions squarely and clearly, individuals just starting to learn can quickly learn how to use the machine and produce different nice results. It is a modern machine that enables even people just starting to knit to make nice, attractive, complex baby blankets without stress. It has a different user-friendly design and concise instructional material, and the machine has evolved in the knitting world.

Firstly, set up the fisherman machine with the manual that came with it, with no mistakes. And make sure that all the essential parts are where they are supposed to be. Follow all the instructions, including the step-by-step instructions in the manual. Then, pick a yarn or material you like and put a thread in through the machine. It has a feeder. Then, pick a stitch design of your choice, the one you like, and you can start to knit. You can start knitting by turning the handle in a steady motion. The machine will then make a scalloped edge automatically for the added flair and watch while the blanket makes a nice shape before your eyes.

The scalloped design makes the material look very nice and charming at the end of the knitting, making it look perfect for giving people a gift they can cherish.

With practice and patience, one can make a nice one-in-town blanket that will be a treasure for many years.

If the person knitting is a professional knitter or just a beginner with a passion for learning the skill, the fisherman scalloped baby blanket knitting machine is the right machine to make nice and attractive blankets with its flexibility and ease of use.

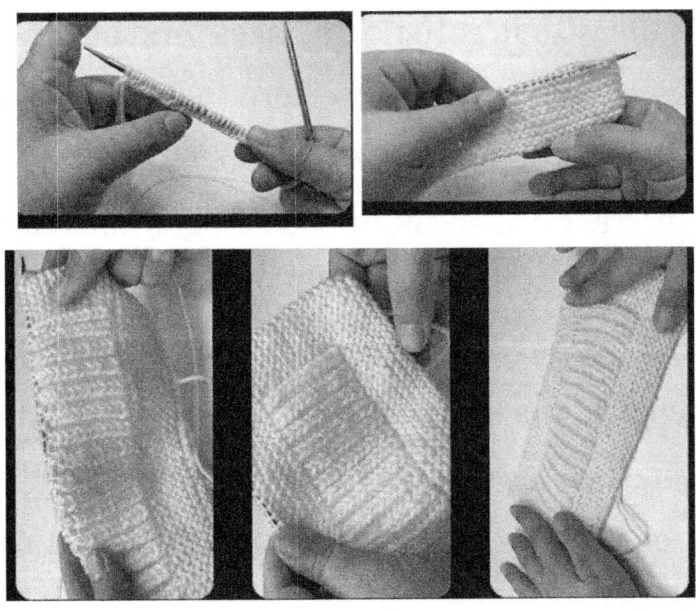

Tips for Achieving the Perfect Rack

The art of knitting has become a pleasure for a very long time, with the rack knitting machine evolving the way people make nice, beautiful, and complex patterns to achieve the perfect results with the innovative machine. Achieving the perfect rack in knitting is a height many people want to attain. Having the right tips and methods, anybody can make an attractive and uniform rack in their knitting work.

One main tip is to use a yarn or material of high quality and appropriate for the work the individual has at hand at all times, and this makes sure that all the stitches on the material are regular, even, and consistent. It also helps the machine work well and not break or snag.

Another thing is paying close attention to the machine's tension while knitting, which is crucial to making a good rack. Always ensure that the tension is very regular, not too tight, and not too loose. It makes work look professional, and oiling and cleaning the machine is always important; it helps avoid any jams or malfunctions.

Also, practicing patience and taking all the time needed to work on a particular project is important. It will result in more peculiar and nice results. Also, do not be scared to experiment with various designs and methods to see and know the full ability of the rack knitting machine.

Another crucial tip is also to learn to close any finished work after it has been completed. Closing helps in the evening out of the inconsistency in the stitches and makes the work look more polished.

Lastly, practice makes perfect. When it involves getting a good rack in knitting, one has to keep practicing and experimenting with different methods until one finds the one that best works. Dedication and patience.

Following these tips, you can achieve stunning creations that showcase your skill and creativity in this timeless craft.

Chapter Two

Fisherman's Rib
Reversible Cable Stitch

The Fisherman's Rib Reversible Cable Stitch Knitting Machine is a recent technology that enables knitters to make complex and nice patterns without stress. It is a classic and flexible tool that adds some texture to any work done, and the tool has advanced technology features that are user-friendly and have evolved over the years. The complex patterns make a thick, cozy material perfect for hats, sweaters, and scarves.

To make a fisherman's rib reversible cable stitch, the knitters must first make a cast on an even number of stitches. This design alternates between a purl and a knit on each row, making a ribbed effect that looks like the scales of a fish. The cables are then made by crossing stitches over one another to make complex braids and twists.

One of the intriguing areas in the fisherman's rib reversible cable stitch is its flexibility. Depending on the material and the needle size, it can look different. Knowing the classic stitch will add more dimensions and insights to a person's work if, the person is a beginner or a professional knitter.

The Fisherman's Rib Reversible Cable Stitch Knitting Machine can make nice, attractive reversible cable stitch designs that were also achievable by professional hand-knitters. Using this tool, a first-time beginner can quickly make professional quality designs and garments.

The machine saves time and energy and opens a new opportunity for knitters. The complex patterns and designs that can be made with the Fisherman's Rib Reversible Cable Stitch Knitting Machine are truly breathtaking.

The Fisherman's Rib Reversible Cable Stitch Knitting Machine is a game-changer for knitters everywhere. Its innovative design and functionality make it a must-have tool for anyone passionate about knitting.

Instructions

The Fisherman's Rib Reversible Cable Stitch is a classic knitting procedure that helps make a fine and attractive textured material. It adds texture and depth to any work. One will need a knitting tool with a rubber attached to make the complex stitch design.

To make a good stitch design, there are some instructions one has to follow attentively:

The first thing to do is to set up the machine for ribbing. To do this, the correct needle and tension will be set up. After that, put your desired even number of stitches and then knit the first row on a plain knit stitch. Do it by knitting the first row in fisherman's rib design, the knit 1, and purl 1 through the back loop across the row. Then, the cable needles needed are set, and we begin to work on the fisherman's rib design by exchanging the purl and the knit stitch on each row. Then, continue to repeat this on each row.

To make a reversible cable twist, slip the two stitches into a cable needle and hold them in front of your work. Then, knit two stitches from the left needle and knit the two stitches from the cable needle. Continue to do this design across the row.

After doing the two rows until you have gotten your desired length, finish up the few rows of the fisherman rib pattern to have a clean and neater edge. By doing this regularly and patiently, someone can make a nice reversible cable stitch without stress.

Continue knitting in this manner until you have reached your desired length. To create the reversible cable effect, twist the cable needles in opposite directions every few rows.

With practice and patience, you can master the art of the Fisherman's Rib Reversible Cable Stitch on your knitting machine and create stunning garments that will impress you.

How to Cross the Cables

Knitting is a relaxing hobby, but it might seem difficult for people just starting. But, with practice, patience, and a few steps, and knowing the procedure, one can make a beautiful design and add some nice texture and dimensions to one's work.

The first thing to do is to read the design instructions carefully and then be familiar with the cable crossings.

Next, look for the stitches that need to be crossed and in which direction they will be crossed.

You will need a cable needle or a double-pointed needle to cross the cables and hold the stitches that want to be crossed. Then, slip the stitches into the cable needle and hold them either in the front of your work or behind. This depends on the direction in which you want to cross the stitch, then knit the next set of stitches as instructed in the design, and then attentively knit the stitches from the cable needle back onto the main needle.

It is important to make sure that you have the correct instruments. The cable needles and double-pointed needles are very important for crossing cables. Then, when working with the cables, it is crucial to note the stitches and follow the design carefully. You can use a stitch marker to help you organize and prevent mistakes.

Next, practice makes perfect! Start with simple cable patterns before attempting more complex designs. Remember to knit at a consistent tension to ensure even results.

By following these tips and practicing regularly, you will soon become confident in crossing cables in your knitting projects. Enjoy the process, and watch as your skills grow!

With practice and patience, you will soon master crossing cables on your knitting machine and create stunning textured designs in your projects.

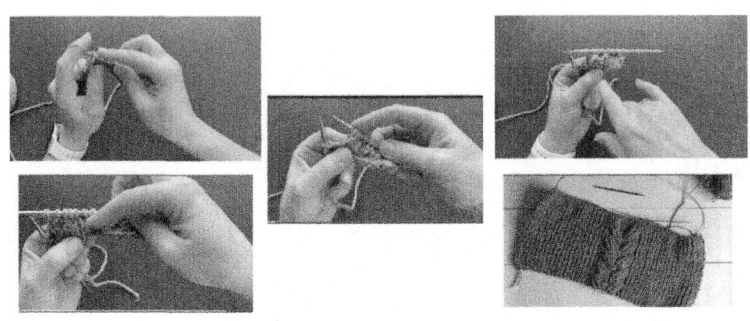

A Simple Machine Knit Hat Pattern

Knitting has evolved and been a craft for many years, with its complex designs and patterns passed through many generations. Still, with advancements in technology, knitting machines have been produced, making work faster and more effective. One simple machine knit hat pattern that is good for people just starting entails using a knitting machine to make a stylish and cozy accessory.

The simple machine knit hat pattern is a one-time and flexible design that has been in the fashion line for many generations. This design features a basic ribbed brim and a cozy stockinette stitch body, which makes it good for beginners and professional knitters.

One of the major beauties of this design is its simplicity and how it functions. The ribbed brim produces a snug fit that keeps the hat in place, while the stockinette gives it a smooth and polished finish. The tool knitting procedure enables quick and effective production, making it ideal work for those looking to make a handmade gift or bulk orders.

The possibilities are endless, whether you knit this hat in a solid color or experiment with stripes or color blocking. With just a few skeins of yarn and basic knitting skills, you can create a stylish and practical accessory that will keep you warm all winter.

Creating a hat using a knitting machine may seem hard, but it can be simple and enjoyable with the right tools and techniques. The first step in creating a hat is picking the right material or yarn and needles for your work. After getting all your materials, set up your knitting machine according to the manufacturer's instructions.

Next, cast the desired number of stitches onto the machine's needle bed. Begin knitting in the round, following the pattern or design you have chosen for your hat. As you continue knitting, periodically check your tension and adjust it to ensure an even and consistent fabric.

Once you have reached the desired length for your hat, bind off the stitches and seam up any remaining openings. Finally, add any embellishments or finishing touches to complete your handmade creation. With practice and patience, anyone can create a beautiful hat using a knitting machine.

With just a few simple steps, you can create a beautiful hat using a knitting machine to keep you warm and stylish all winter.

Chapter Three

The Bulky Gauge Machine

In the early years of the 19th century, the making of the bulky gauge machine evolved into the textile industry. This innovative machine enabled faster and more effective production of knitted materials, making it possible to make larger and more complex designs than ever before. The bulky gauge machine was a life-changer for manufacturers, enabling them to meet the growing demand for high-quality knitwear. The Bulky Gauge Knitting Machine is a revolutionary machine that has changed the knitting world. This machine allows for creating large, chunky knits in a fraction of the time it would take to hand knit them. The bulky gauge knitting machine is good for creating nice, cozy blankets, warm sweaters, and stylish scarves without stress.

With the advancement of technology and precision engineering, the bulky gauge machine became a staple in textile factories worldwide. Its profound impact on the industry led to increased productivity and profitability for businesses that adopted this cutting-edge technology.

In recent times, the legacy of the bulky gauge machine lives on in modern knitting machines that continue to push boundaries and redefine what is possible in textile production. Its influence in the textile industry can be seen in every knitted garment we wear, a testament to its enduring importance in shaping the world of fashion and manufacturing.

One of the advantages of this machine is its efficiency. With the capacity to knit quickly and accurately, people can quickly make high-quality pieces without wasting time. Also, the bulky gauge knitting machine offers versatility and flexibility in stitch designs, allowing for endless creativity and customization.

In summary, the bulky gauge knitting machine has become a staple tool for knitters of all skill levels. Its ease of use, efficiency, effectiveness, and versatility make it a must-have for anyone looking to expand their knitting capacity.

The Standard Gauge Machine

The Standard Gauge Machine evolved the world of transportation with its uniform track width, allowing for seamless travel between different regions and countries. Made in the early 19th century, this innovation standardized railway systems and greatly improved efficiency and safety in the industry. The Standard Gauge Knitting Machine revolutionized the textile industry with efficiency and effectiveness. It was developed in the early 20th century. This innovative machine quickly became a staple in garment manufacturing due to its ability to produce high-quality knitted fabrics at a rapid pace.

The introduction of the Standard Gauge Machine led to a boom in railway construction, connecting cities and towns like never before. It facilitated the movement of goods and people on an unimaginable scale, fueling economic growth and development across nations.

The Standard Gauge Machine became a very important part of modern infrastructure, shaping how we travel and transport goods to this day. Its impact on the community cannot be overemphasized, as it continues to play a very important part in global trade and connectivity.

One of the important features of the Standard Gauge Knitting Machine is its standardized needle spacing, which allows for consistent and uniform stitches. This ensures a superior finished product and reduces the production time significantly compared to hand knitting.

The versatility of this tool cannot be compared and unmatched, and it can also be used to make a wide range of knitted items, from fragile lace designs to thick winter sweaters. Its ease of use and reliability have made it a favorite among both those using it as a leisure and professional knitter.

The Standard Gauge Machine is a testament to human ingenuity and innovation, forever changing how we move from place to place.

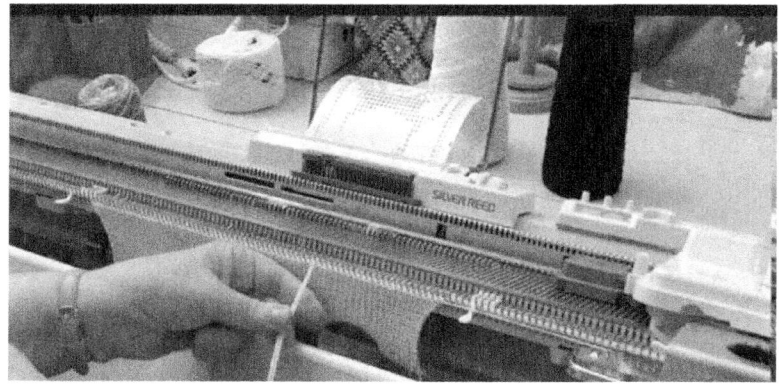

Lace Circular Doily Dish Rag Pattern

The lace circular doily dish rag pattern is a good and nice design that has been passed from one generation to another. Its complex details and delicate lacework make it a beautiful addition to any home decor. The circular shape of the doily adds a touch of sophistication to any table setting, while the absorbent qualities of the dish rag make it practical for everyday use.

With much care and attention to every detail, this pattern requires skill and patience to create. Each stitch is carefully placed to achieve the intricate lace design that sets this doily apart. Whether used as a decorative accent or as a functional dish rag, the lace circular doily pattern will impress all who see it.

The circular shape of the doily adds a nice touch to any table or countertop, while the knitted texture provides a soft surface for drying dishes or wiping up spills. The intricate lace pattern requires careful attention to detail and precision in each stitch, making it a challenging yet rewarding project for experienced knitters.

In conclusion, the lace circular doily dish rag pattern is a classic design that combines beauty and functionality in one stunning piece. Knitting has long been a beloved craft, passed down through generations as a way to create beautiful and functional items. One such item that showcases the artistry and skill of knitting is the lace circular doily dish rag pattern. This intricate design combines delicate lacework with practicality, making it a decorative and useful household item.

Chapter Four
Types of Machines

Plastic Bed Machines

These machines are lightweight and affordable, making them an excellent choice for beginners. They are easy to transport and store, making them convenient for those with limited space.

Functionality

Plastic bed knitting machines function similarly to traditional ones but use plastic needles. The machine features a carriage that holds the yarn and moves across the bed, allowing the needles to knit the yarn into fabric. The plastic needles are designed to be durable and smooth to ensure seamless knitting.

Advantages

One of the main advantages of plastic bed knitting machines is their lightweight construction, making them easily portable and suitable for home use.

Additionally, these machines are often more affordable than their metal bed counterparts, making them accessible to a wider range of users. They also require minimal maintenance and are relatively easy to operate, making them ideal for beginners in machine knitting.

ApplicatioPlastic bed knitting machines can create various knitted items such as scarves, hats, blankets, and even garments. They offer versatility in stitch patterns and can accommodate different types of yarn, allowing users to explore various creative possibilities.

Maintenance
While plastic bed knitting machines are generally low-maintenance, keeping them clean and free from dust or debris that could affect their performance is important. Regular oiling of moving parts may also be necessary to ensure smooth operation.

Metal Bed Machines
These machines are more durable and sturdy than plastic bed machines, providing better support for

larger projects. They are ideal for those who plan to use their machines frequently.

Electronic Machines: These machines offer advanced features like programmable stitch patterns and automatic row-by-row knitting. They can be more expensive but provide greater control and versatility.

Ribbing Attachment: This attachment is used for knitting narrow bands, such as cuffs, collars, and hems. It can be added to most circular knitting machines.

Advantages of Metal Bed Machines

Metal bed machines offer several advantages in various industries:

Durability: Metal bed machines are known for their durability and strength, making them suitable for heavy-duty applications. They can withstand high loads and provide long-term reliability.

Precision: These machines can achieve high levels of precision in manufacturing processes. This is crucial for aerospace, automotive, and medical equipment manufacturing industries, where precision is paramount.

Versatility: Metal bed machines can be used for various applications, including milling, turning, drilling, and grinding. This versatility makes them valuable assets in manufacturing facilities.

Stability: The rigid structure of metal bed machines provides stability during machining operations, leading to consistent and accurate results.

Vibration Dampening: Metal bed machines are effective at dampening vibrations, which is essential for maintaining the integrity of the workpiece and achieving quality surface finishes.

Longevity: When properly maintained, metal bed machines have a long lifespan, offering businesses a good return on investment.

Rigidity: The inherent rigidity of metal bed machines allows for heavy cutting and machining operations without compromising the structural integrity of the machine.

Disadvantages of Metal Bed Machines

While metal bed machines offer numerous advantages, there are also some disadvantages to consider:

Cost: Metal bed machines tend to be more expensive than their counterparts due to the materials and construction required for their robustness and stability.

Weight: The sturdy construction of metal bed machines contributes to their weight, making them less portable and requiring substantial floor space in manufacturing facilities.

Complexity: Some metal bed machines may have complex designs and structures, making maintenance and repairs more challenging.

Limited Accessibility: The design of metal bed machines may limit accessibility to certain workpiece areas, especially compared to open-bed or gantry-style machines.

Setup Time: Using metal bed machines for different machining tasks may require more time and effort than other machines.

Transportation: Due to their weight and size, transporting metal bed machines can be logistically challenging and may require specialized equipment.

In conclusion, while metal bed machines offer durability, precision, versatility, stability, vibration dampening, longevity, and rigidity, they also come with considerations regarding cost, weight, complexity, limited accessibility, setup time, and transportation challenges.

Chapter Five

Electronic Machines

What is an electronic knitting machine?

An electronic knitting machine is a type of computerized knitting machine that uses electronic components and digital technology to create knitted fabrics. These machines are designed to automate the knitting process, making it faster, more precise, and more efficient than traditional manual knitting methods. They are commonly used in the textile industry to mass-produce garments and other knitted items.

How do electronic knitting machines work?

Electronic knitting machines operate using a combination of electronic and mechanical components. The main parts of an electronic knitting machine include the control unit, the carriage, the bed, and the needles. The control unit is responsible for managing the machine's various functions, such as controlling the movement of the carriage and needles. The carriage contains the yarn feeders and the knitting needles, responsible for creating the knitted fabric. The bed holds the work in progress and supports the knitting process.

Knitting with an electronic machine begins with loading the yarn onto the machine. The yarn is then fed through the yarn feeders, controlled by the control unit. As the carriage moves back and forth across the bed, the needles knit the yarn into a fabric according to the programmed pattern. The finished fabric is removed from the bed and wound onto a take-up roll.

Advantages of Electronic Knitting Machines

Electronic knitting machines offer several advantages over traditional manual knitting techniques:

Increased Efficiency: These machines can induce knitted fabrics much faster than manual knitting, leading to higher production output and reduced lead times.

Precision and Consistency: The computerized control system ensures uniform stitch formation and pattern accuracy, eliminating variations commonly associated with manual knitting.

Complex Design Capabilities: Electronic knitting machines can execute intricate patterns, textures, and colorwork with ease, allowing for greater design versatility and creativity.

Reduced Labor Intensity: Automation minimizes the need for extensive manual labor, lowering production costs and labor requirements.

Customization Options: Users can easily modify design elements and parameters to create customized fabrics tailored to specific requirements.

Integration with CAD Systems: Many electronic knitting machines are compatible with computer-aided design (CAD) software, enabling seamless integration of digital designs into the knitting process.

Applications of Electronic Knitting Machines

The versatility of electronic knitting machines has led to their widespread use across various industries:

Fashion and Apparel: These machines are extensively utilized to produce knitted garments, including sweaters, dresses, scarves, and accessories.

Textile Manufacturing: Electronic knitting machines manufacture diverse textile products such as upholstery fabrics, technical textiles, and industrial materials.

Prototyping and Sampling: Designers and manufacturers use electronic knitting machines to prototype and sample new fabric designs before full-scale production.

Custom Textile Production: They enable on-demand production of custom textiles for niche markets or personalized products.

Research and Development: Electronic knitting machines play a crucial role in textile research and development activities aimed at exploring innovative fabric structures and properties

Rubbing Attachment
Understanding Ribbing Attachments
Ribbing attachments are tools commonly used in the sewing industry to create ribbed patterns on various fabrics. These attachments are designed for sewing machines and are available in different sizes and shapes to accommodate specific fabrics and designs.

Types of Ribbing Attachments

There are several types of ribbing attachments, including:

Flatbed Ribbing Attachment: This attachment is used for knitted fabrics and creates a flat ribbed pattern. It is suitable for creating cuffs, collars, and waistbands.

Circular Ribbing Attachment: This attachment is designed for circular knitting and creates a tubular ribbed pattern. It is ideal for creating socks, leggings, and other tight-fitting garments.

Double-Layer Ribbing Attachment: As the name suggests, this attachment is used for sewing double-layered ribbed patterns. It is suitable for creating thicker garments like tights and leggings.

Zipper Ribbing Attachment: This attachment is specifically designed for sewing ribbed patterns around zippers. It helps to create a seamless finish and prevents the zipper from pulling the fabric.

How to Use a Ribbing Attachment

Using a ribbing attachment is relatively simple, but it requires some practice to master. Here are the general steps to follow:

Prepare the Fabric: Choose the appropriate ribbing attachment for the fabric and design you want to create. Cut the fabric to the desired size and fold it in half or the required shape.

Attach the rib attachment: Follow your sewing machine's instructions to attach the rib attachment. Ensure the attachment is securely fastened and properly aligned with the sewing machine's needle.

Set the Stitch Length: Adjust the stitch length on your sewing machine to the recommended setting for the ribbing attachment you are using. This will ensure that the stitches are evenly spaced and the ribbed pattern is consistent.

Sew the Ribbed Pattern: Place the fabric on the sewing machine and start sewing. Follow the manufacturer's instructions for the specific ribbing attachment you are using to create the desired ribbed pattern.

Remove the rib attachment: Carefully detach the rib attachment from the sewing machine and store it safely once you have finished sewing.

Knitting Basics

Knitting is a craft that involves creating fabric by interlocking loops of yarn with knitting needles. It is a popular hobby that allows individuals to create a wide range of items, from clothing and accessories to home décor. Understanding the basics of knitting is essential for beginners looking to start their knitting journey.

Materials Needed for Knitting

To start knitting, you will need a few basic materials. These include:

Yarn: Yarn comes in various colors, textures, and weights. Choosing the right yarn for your project is important based on fiber content, thickness, and color.

Knitting Needles: Knitting needles are available in different sizes and materials, such as wood, metal, and plastic. The size of the needles will depend on the weight of the yarn and the desired tension of the finished piece.

Scissors: A pair of scissors is necessary for cutting the yarn at the end of a project or when changing colors.

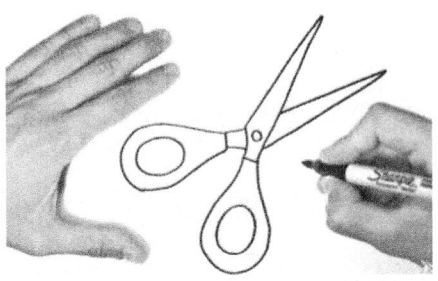

Tapestry Needle: This type of needle is used for weaving loose ends and sewing seams together.

Measuring Tape: A measuring tape is useful for checking gauges and taking measurements for sizing.

Stitch Markers: Stitch markers help keep track of specific points in your knitting, such as the beginning of a round in circular knitting.

Basic Knitting Techniques

There are two fundamental knitting techniques: knit stitch and purl stitch. These stitches form the foundation for all knitted fabric.

Knit Stitch: The knit stitch creates a smooth surface on the right side of the fabric and forms a series of interlocking loops on the wrong side.

Purl Stitch: The purl stitch creates a bumpy texture on the right side of the fabric and a smooth surface on the wrong side.

By combining these two basic stitches in various patterns and sequences, knitters can create endless textures, designs, and patterns in their projects.

Getting Started with Knitting

For beginners, it is recommended to start with simple projects such as scarves or dishcloths to practice basic stitches and techniques. Learning how to cast on stitches, knit, purl, and bind off will provide a solid foundation for more advanced projects in the future.

Numerous resources are available for learning how to knit, including online tutorials, books, and local knitting classes or workshops. Additionally, joining knitting communities or clubs can provide valuable support and guidance for beginners as they embark on their knitting journey.

Knitting Gauge Explained: The knitting gauge is the number of stitches and rows per inch or centimeter. Ensuring the finished project matches the desired size and is compatible with the chosen yarn and needle size is essential.

Types of Gauges on Knitting Machines

a. Bulky Gauge: This gauge is used for knitting thicker yarns and larger projects, such as blankets and sweaters.

The phrase "bulky gauge" in knitting describes using larger needles and thicker yarn to create a looser, more open fabric. This gauge is frequently used to make warm and comforting garments like blankets, scarves, and sweaters. Because of the larger stitches and faster knitting speed, the bulky gauge is popular for winter clothing and home decor projects. Following the suggested needle size and gauge listed on the yarn label or pattern, instructions are crucial when using bulky gauge yarn. It is ensured that the piece will have the desired drape and texture by using the appropriate needle size. Bulky gauge yarn can knit up quickly and produce warm, substantial fabrics, making it a rewarding yarn. It's a well-liked option for people who want to make cozy, homey things with a more carefree, informal vibe.

b. **Mid-Gauge**: This gauge is suitable for knitting medium-weight yarns and projects, such as cardigans and dresses. Concerning needle spacing, mid-gauge knitting machines have a special place in the machine knitting industry, sandwiched between bulky gauge and standard gauge machines. While bulky gauge machines have a needle spacing of 9 mm or more, and standard gauge machines typically have a needle spacing of 4 point 5 mm, mid-gauge machines usually have a needle spacing of 6 point 5 mm to 7 mm and are appropriate for finer yarns. When it comes to yarn weights, mid-gauge machines can handle a greater variety than standard or bulky machines because of this needle spacing. Their versatility allows them to create a wide range of knitted fabrics, as they can handle yarns from sport weight to DK (double knitting) weight more effectively. Using yarns that are neither too fine nor too chunky, knitters can balance warmth and drape in their finished garments using mid-gauge machines. The ability to create fabrics with a medium density that can be used for a variety of clothing and accessories is one of the benefits of mid-gauge knitting. Mid-gauge knitting machines enable knitters to produce garments with a well-balanced thickness and structure, such as cardigans, sweaters, scarves, and hats. Furthermore, knitters can experiment with various textures and designs because mid-gauge machines frequently have a variety of stitch patterns and features. Certain models might have options for lace knitting, patterning, or even automatic color changes to encourage creativity.

c. Standard Gauge: This gauge knits fine yarns and delicate projects like scarves and baby clothes. The needle spacing on standard gauge knitting machines is 4.5 mm, meaning that every needle is placed 4.5 mm apart from the needles next to it. Fine stitches and complex patterns can be made with this close needle spacing.

Yarn Compatibility: Finer yarn weights, such as sport weight or lace weight, are optimized for use with standard gauge machines. These yarns create lightweight fabrics with a delicate drape, perfect for accessories and clothing that need a finer texture.

Features of the Fabric: Fabrics made with standard gauge machines typically have tight stitches and a smooth, uniform texture. You can use them to make clothing with lacework, fine details, and complex stitch patterns. The end products are frequently breathable, lightweight, and opulent-feeling fabrics.

Versatility: Standard gauge machines have great versatility despite their small needle spacing. They are useful for knitting many different types of clothing, such as cardigans, sweaters, shawls, scarves, and even socks. Knitters can create various looks and styles by experimenting with stitch patterns, colorwork methods, and garment constructions.

Proficiency: Utilizing a standard gauge knitting machine requires expertise and meticulousness, particularly when handling delicate yarns and elaborate designs. Learning the skills necessary to achieve consistent tension may be difficult for beginners.

Advantages of Knitting Gauge:

Proper Sizing: One of the primary advantages of paying attention to knitting gauge is that it ensures the finished knitted item matches the intended size. By matching the pattern's specified gauge, knitters can create garments or accessories that fit as intended.

Yarn Substitution: Understanding knitting gauge allows knitters to substitute yarns in patterns while achieving the correct sizing. Knitters can use different yarn weights without compromising the final product's dimensions by adjusting needle sizes to match the pattern's gauge.

Professional Finish: The correct gauge produces a professional-looking finish for knitted items. Consistent tension and stitch size contribute to a polished appearance in the finished project.

Pattern Accuracy: Following the recommended gauge ensures that the stitch pattern's design elements appear as intended. This is particularly important for intricate stitch patterns or colorwork designs.

Efficiency: Paying attention to gauge from the beginning of a project can save time and effort by preventing the need for extensive adjustments or re-knitting due to incorrect sizing.

Disadvantages of Knitting Gauge:

Time-Consuming: Achieving the correct gauge may require swatching with different needle sizes and yarns, which can be time-consuming, especially for larger projects.

Limited Yarn Options: Some knitters may find that achieving the correct gauge with a specific yarn requires using a limited selection of needle sizes, limiting their ability to choose from various needle sizes for different effects freely.

Frustration for Beginners: For novice knitters, understanding and achieving gauge can be challenging and may lead to frustration if not achieved accurately.

Additional Calculations: When substituting yarn or adjusting gauge, knitters may need to make additional calculations to ensure that pattern instructions align with their modified gauge.

In conclusion, while paying attention to knitting gauge has several advantages, such as ensuring proper sizing, allowing yarn substitution, and contributing to a professional finish, it also comes with potential disadvantages, such as being time-consuming, limiting yarn options, and causing frustration for beginners.

Chapter Six

Circular Knitting Machine Patterns for DIY Products

DIY Headband

A simple pattern for knitting a headband using a circular knitting machine.

Loom Knit Holiday Bag: A more advanced pattern for creating a stylish bag using a circular knitting machine. Addi Boho Towel Ring: A unique pattern for knitting a decorative towel ring that adds a touch of elegance to any bathroom.

Maci Beanie: A cozy beanie pattern suitable for beginners, perfect for keeping hands warm during colder months
.

Colorful Twist Headband: A fun and colorful headband pattern that adds color to any outfit.

DIY Rainbow Wall Hanging: A visually appealing wall-hanging pattern that adds a touch of creativity to any room.
Brioche Stitch

Advantages of DIY Headbands

DIY headbands offer several advantages, making them popular for individuals looking to create accessories. Some of the key advantages include:

Customization: One of the primary benefits of DIY headbands is the ability to customize them according to personal preferences. Individuals can choose their preferred colors, patterns, and materials, allowing for a unique and personalized accessory.

Cost-Effective: Creating headbands at home can be a cost-effective alternative to purchasing them from stores. Individuals can save money using readily available materials or repurposing existing items while achieving stylish headbands.

Creativity and Self-Expression: DIY headbands provide an avenue for creativity and self-expression. Individuals can experiment with different designs, embellishments, and techniques, allowing them to showcase their unique style and personality through their accessories.

Sustainability: Making headbands at home aligns with sustainable practices by reducing the reliance on mass-produced accessories. Individuals can contribute to environmental conservation efforts by using recycled or eco-friendly materials.

Therapeutic and Relaxing: Engaging in DIY headband projects can be relaxing. It offers a creative outlet that can help reduce stress and anxiety while providing a sense of accomplishment upon completing the project.

Disadvantages of DIY Headbands

While DIY headbands offer numerous advantages, there are also some potential disadvantages to consider:

Time-Consuming: Creating DIY headbands may require a significant time investment, especially for individuals new to crafting or sewing. Selecting materials, designing, and assembling the headbands can be time-consuming.

Skill and Expertise Required: Certain DIY headband designs may necessitate specific crafting skills or expertise in sewing, knitting, or other techniques. Individuals without experience in these areas may face challenges in achieving the desired results.

Quality Variability: The quality of DIY headbands may vary based on individual crafting abilities and the materials used. Sometimes, homemade headbands may not match the durability and finish of professionally manufactured ones.

Limited Resources: Access to a wide range of materials and tools may be limited for some individuals, impacting their ability to create diverse or intricate headband designs.

Initial Investment: While DIY headbands can be cost-effective in the long run, initial investment may be required to purchase crafting supplies and tools, which could deter some individuals from pursuing this hobby. Variations of the Brioche Stitch: The brioche stitch can be knitted in various ways, such as the classic brioche stitch, the two-color brioche stitch, and the cable brioche stitch.

How the Brioche Stitch is Knitted: The brioche stitch is a technique that involves working with two strands of yarn at once, creating a soft and warm fabric. It is a more advanced stitch but can be mastered with practice.

Teardrop Stitch

Interweave Knits: Interweave Knits is a magazine and online resource that offers patterns, techniques, and inspiration for knitters of all skill levels. It was used to find advanced circular knitting machine patterns, such as the loom knit holiday bag and the DIY rainbow wall hanging.

Loom Knit Holiday Bag

This is a type of bag made out of knitting. Here are some steps to consider to neat a bag of this kind.

Assemble the supplies: a round loom (size will vary depending on the size desired for a bag), holiday-colored yarn, loom hook, yarn needle, scissors, and any embellishments you wish to add.

Select Stitch: Choose a stitch design that works well for your bag. Beginners can start with simple knit or purl stitches, but you can experiment with more intricate ones for more texture. To begin knitting, cast a few stitches onto the loom. Knit rows in the pattern of your choice until the bag reaches the desired height. Do not forget to allow sufficient yarn for the drawstring closure at the top of the bag.

Shape the Bag: Work in equal amounts of stitches around the last few rows to make a flat bottom for the bag. The bag will take on a square or rectangular shape as a result.

Bind Off: Join your stitches to create your bag's desired height and shape. This will hold the bag's top and prepare it for finishing. Last touches: trim extra yarn and weave in any loose ends. Your holiday bag can be adorned with buttons, beads, or ribbons if you'd like.

Make a drawstring: Crochet or knit a drawstring using the same yarn as your bag or a contrasting color. A yarn needle should be used to thread it through the top of your bag. Final Adjustments: Pull the drawstring tight to seal the bag's top. To hold the drawstring in place, tie knots at both ends.

Enjoy Your Bag: Now that your loom-knit holiday bag is ready to use, fill it with festive treats, gifts, or other goodies to help spread the holiday spirit. Try it: Don't be hesitant to try out new things.

Addi Boho Towel Ring

To make an Addi Boho Towel Ring, you'll need a towel ring, yarn in the colors of your choice, a crochet hook, and an Addi Express Knitting Machine.

How to make it: Assemble your Addi Express Knitting Machine following the manufacturer's instructions to set it up. Make that a stable surface where it is firmly attached.

 Pick Yarn: Choose your yarn in the colors you want. Though you can choose colors and yarn types, boho-style designs typically feature earthy tones and natural fibers.

Start Knitting: Using the Addi Express, begin knitting a tube using the colors of yarn you have selected. Work with a basic stockinette stitch or try other patterns to keep things simple.

Incorporate Texture: If you want your knitting to have a bohemian vibe, add some texture. This can be achieved by switching up the kinds of yarn (e.g., G. adding fringe or adding tiny knitted or crocheted embellishments., using a thick-and-thin yarn. To create a loop, bind off your stitches after knitting a tube long enough to fit around your towel ring. To sew the ends together, leave a tail of yarn.

Attach Towel Ring: Place the towel ring close to one end of the knitted tube and thread it through. Make sure the ring is firmly and centrally placed.

Join Ends: Use the knitted tube's ends to create a loop by sewing them with a crochet hook and the leftover yarn tail. Ensure that the seam is neat and safe.

Lasting Details: Cut off any extra yarn and tidy up Check for excess yarn; this is the final stage of checking the details.

Maci Beanie

Knitting a Maci beanie involves creating a cozy and stylish hat using specific techniques and patterns. The Maci beanie is known for its textured stitches, often featuring cables or other intricate designs. To knit a Maci beanie, follow a pattern that outlines the required stitches, yarn type, and needle size. Additionally, understanding basic knitting techniques such as casting on, knitting, purling, and decreasing stitches is essential for successfully creating a Maci beanie.

To begin knitting a Maci beanie, you will need to gather the necessary materials, including yarn in the color of your choice, appropriately sized knitting needles, a cable needle if the pattern includes cables, and a tapestry needle for finishing. It's important to select a yarn that complements the desired texture and warmth of the beanie. Once your materials are ready, you can start casting on the required number of stitches as specified in the pattern.

Following the pattern instructions, you will knit the beanie's body using the designated stitch pattern. Depending on the chosen design, this may involve working in rounds or rows. If the pattern includes cables, you will use a cable needle to cross stitches and create a distinctive cable motif. As you progress through the pattern, you will systematically shape the beanie crown by decreasing stitches until only a few remain.

You will need yarn in the desired color, scissors, knitting needles matching the yarn weight, and a tapestry needle to knit a Maci Beanie. To get you started, here's a basic pattern:

Gauge Swatch: To find your stitches per inch, start by knitting a gauge swatch. This will guarantee that the beanie you make fits well.

Cast On: After figuring out your gauge, cast on the number of stitches needed to achieve your desired size. Depending on your gauge and preferred fit, you may begin with a standard adult-size beanie with 80–100 stitches.

Ribbing: For stretchiness, start with a ribbed brim. For a timeless style, use a k1, p1 ribbing pattern. Knit to desired brim length or about 1-2 inches in ribbing.

Body: For the beanie's body, change from ribbing to stockinette stitch (knit all stitches on right side rows, purl all stitches on wrong side rows). Knit the hat until it reaches your desired length or about 7-8 inches from the cast-on edge.

Crown Decreases: You will need to decrease stitches to shape the beanie's crown gradually. A simple decrease pattern follows Row 1: Knit 6, knit 2 together, and repeat to the end of the row. Row 2: Work every stitch. Continue these two rows, decreasing by one stitch every other row, until you have about 8–12 stitches remaining.

Closing: Cut the yarn, making sure to leave a long tail. To close the beanie's crown, thread the tail onto a tapestry needle and pull tightly through the remaining stitches.

Colorful twist headband

A colorful twist headband is a stylish and versatile accessory that adds color and flair to any outfit. These headbands are typically made from a stretchy fabric and feature a twisted design at the front, creating an eye-catching and fashionable look. They come in various colors and patterns, making them suitable for casual outings and formal events.

Features of Colorful Twist Headbands

Colorful twist headbands are known for their unique design and practicality. The twisted front detail adds visual interest and dimension to the headband, making it stand out as a fashion statement. The stretchy nature of the fabric ensures a comfortable and secure fit for different head sizes, making them suitable for adults and children. The available colors and patterns allow individuals to express their style and coordinate the headband with different outfits.

Versatility and Styling Options

One of the key advantages of colorful twist headbands is their versatility. They can be worn with various hairstyles, including loose hair, ponytails, or buns, making them suitable for different hair lengths and textures. Whether it's a casual day out, a workout session, or a special occasion, these headbands can complement different looks and add a playful touch to any ensemble. Furthermore, they are often lightweight and easy to pack, making them convenient for travel or on-the-go styling.

Where to Find Colorful Twist Headbands

Colorful twist headbands can be found in various retail outlets, including fashion accessory stores, department stores, online marketplaces, and specialty boutiques. Many brands offer these headbands in assorted color palettes and designs, allowing customers to choose options that align with their preferences.

DIY Rainbow Wall Hanging

Gather materials: You will need the following items:

Fabric or felt in various rainbow colors (red, orange, yellow, green, blue, and purple)

Scissors

Sewing machine or hot glue gun

Thread or glue sticks that match the fabric colors

A long string or ribbon for hanging

A ruler or measuring tape

Pins or fabric weights

Measure and cut fabric pieces: a. Determine the size of the rainbow wall hanging you want to create. b. Measure and cut the fabric or felt into rectangular or square shapes. The size of each piece can vary, but ensure they are consistent within each color of the rainbow.

Create a rainbow pattern: Arrange the fabric pieces in a rainbow order (red, orange, yellow, green, blue, and purple). b. Pin or weigh down the fabric pieces to keep them in place while you work on the next step.

Sew or glue the fabric pieces together: a. If using a sewing machine, sew the fabric pieces together in a straight line along one of the shorter edges, starting with red and ending with purple. b. If using a hot glue gun, apply a glue line along one of the shorter edges of each fabric piece and press them together, ensuring the colors match the rainbow order. Allow the glue to dry completely.

Attach the hanging string or ribbon: Measure and cut a long string or ribbon long enough to hang the rainbow wall on your desired wall. b. Fold the string or ribbon in half to create a loop. c. Sew or glue the loop to the top of the rainbow, ensuring it is secure and centered.

Hang the rainbow wall hanging: Locate the appropriate spot where you want to hang the rainbow. b. Use a nail or adhesive hook to secure the string or ribbon loop to the wall. c. Adjust the rainbow's position to ensure it is straight and centered.

Brioche Stitch

Brioche stitch is a knitting technique that creates a lofty, reversible fabric with a unique texture. Its distinctive ribbed appearance characterizes it and is often used to create warm and cozy garments such as scarves, hats, and sweaters. The stitch is achieved by working yarn over and slipping stitches together, creating a squishy, cushioned fabric.

How to Knit Brioche Stitch

To knit the brioche stitch, you must use a special technique that involves working with two colors of yarn and slipping stitches. The basic steps for knitting brioche stitch include casting on an even number of stitches, setting up the first row with a setup row, and then alternating between knit and purl stitches while slipping certain stitches with yarn overs to create the characteristic brioche texture.

Applications of Brioche Stitch

Brioche stitch is commonly used to create knitted items such as scarves, cowls, shawls, and sweaters. Its reversible nature makes it ideal for projects where both sides of the fabric are visible. Brioche stitch can be combined with other knitting techniques to create intricate patterns and designs.

Benefits of Brioche Stitch

One of the main benefits of brioche stitch is its warmth and squishiness due to the double-layered fabric it creates. This makes it particularly suitable for cold-weather accessories and garments. Additionally, the reversible nature of brioche stitch adds versatility to knitted pieces, allowing for different looks on each side.

Challenges of Knitting Brioche Stitch

While brioche stitch produces beautiful results, it can be more complex than traditional knitting techniques, especially for beginners. Keeping track of the different yarn-overs and slipped stitches may require extra attention and concentration. However, with practice, knitters can master this unique stitch and enjoy the stunning textures it produces.

Variations of the Brioche Stitch

The brioche stitch is a beautiful and versatile knitting technique that creates a lofty, reversible fabric with a unique texture. The brioche stitch has several variations, each offering its distinct look and feel. These variations can involve different combinations of knit, purl, and yarn-over stitches and working with multiple colors. Here are some common variations of the brioche stitch:

Basic Brioche Stitch: The basic brioche stitch involves working a combination of a slipped stitch yarn over (sl1yo) and a brioche knit (brk) or brioche purl (brp) stitch. This creates a ribbed fabric with a distinctive texture.

Two-Color Brioche Stitch: In two-color brioche, two contrasting yarns create a stunning reversible fabric with a deeply textured appearance. This variation often involves working with two colors in a row and using specific techniques to create intricate color patterns.

Fisherman's Rib: While not technically a brioche stitch, fisherman's rib is often considered a variation due to its similarities. This technique creates a plush, stretchy fabric that resembles brioche but is achieved through different methods, such as knitting into the row below.

Syncopated Brioche: Syncopated brioche introduces additional complexity by alternating the placement of the slipped stitches and yarn-overs, resulting in an interplay of textures and colors that can be visually striking.

Honeycomb Brioche: This variation creates a honeycomb-like texture by combining brioche stitches with slipped stitches worked over multiple rows. The result is a deeply textured fabric that adds visual interest to any project.

Garter Stitch Brioche: Garter stitch brioche combines garter stitch with the brioche technique to produce a squishy, reversible fabric showcasing knit and purl textures.

Tuck Stitch Brioche: Tuck stitch brioche incorporates tucking stitches behind others to create raised motifs within the fabric. This variation adds dimension and visual appeal to brioche knitting projects.

How the Brioche Stitch is Knitted

The brioche stitch is a beautiful and unique knitting technique that creates a lofty, reversible fabric with a lovely texture. It is often used to create scarves, shawls, and other garments. To knit the brioche stitch, you will need to follow these steps:

Step 1: Cast On Begin by casting on an even number of stitches using your preferred method. The brioche stitch requires an even number of stitches to work properly.

Step 2: Setup Row For the setup row, knit one stitch, yarn over, and slip 1 across the entire row. This will create the foundation for the brioche stitch pattern.

Step 3: First Pass On the first pass of the brioche stitch pattern, you will work with two different yarns. Hold one yarn in your left hand and the other in your right. Begin by knitting the next stitch with its accompanying yarn from the setup row. Then, yarn over slip 1 across the row.

Step 4: Second Pass: you will work with just one yarn for the second pass. Slip the first stitch purlwise, yarn over, and slip 1 across the row.

Step 5: Repeat. Continue alternating between the first and second passes to create the brioche stitch pattern. The result will be a plush, reversible fabric with a distinctive ribbed texture.

Step 6: Bind Off When you have reached your desired length, bind off your stitches using a stretchy bind-off method to maintain the elasticity of the brioche stitch.

Following these steps, you can create a beautifully textured fabric using the brioche stitch technique.

Teardrop Stitch

The teardrop stitch is a decorative embroidery stitch that resembles a teardrop shape. It is commonly used in hand embroidery to create intricate and delicate designs on fabric. The stitch is formed by creating a series of small straight stitches that converge at a central point, forming the teardrop shape. This stitch can create floral motifs, leaves, and other organic shapes in embroidery projects.

How to Create the Teardrop Stitch

To create the teardrop stitch, follow these steps:

Bring the needle up through the fabric at the starting point of the teardrop shape.

Make a small straight stitch in the desired direction of the teardrop, ensuring that the length matches the desired length of the teardrop.

Here's how to do the teardrop stitch:

Start by bringing your needle up through the fabric at the starting point of your teardrop shape.

Insert the needle back into the fabric slightly to the side of the starting point, forming the narrow end of the teardrop.

Bring the needle up again at a point further along the teardrop shape, forming the wider end of the teardrop.

Insert the needle back into the fabric at the same point where you started the wide end of the teardrop, but slightly to the side, creating a curve.

Continue this process, alternating sides as you move along the teardrop shape until you reach the desired length.

To finish the stitch, bring the needle to the back of the fabric and secure the thread.

Remember to keep your stitches consistent in length and spacing for a neat and uniform appearance. Practice on a scrap fabric until you feel comfortable with the technique.

Abbreviations in Knitting

In knitting, abbreviations are commonly used to make patterns more concise and easier to read. These abbreviations represent specific stitches, techniques, or instructions. Understanding these abbreviations is essential for following knitting patterns accurately. Here are some common knitting abbreviations and their meanings:

K: Knit

P: Purl

YO: Yarn over

SSK: Slip, slip, knit

K2tog: Knit two together

P2tog: Purl two together

PM: Place marker

SM: Slip marker

RS: Right side

WS: Wrong side

These are just a few examples of the many knitting abbreviations used in patterns. Each pattern may have its unique set of abbreviations, so it's important to refer to the key or legend provided in the pattern to understand the specific abbreviations used.

Instructions in Knitting

Knitting instructions can vary widely depending on the pattern and the desired outcome. However, some common instructions appear frequently in knitting patterns. These instructions dictate how to perform specific stitches or techniques to create the desired fabric. Some common knitting instructions include:

Cast on: This is the foundation of any knitting project, where stitches are added to the needle before beginning the main pattern.

Knit: This basic stitch creates a smooth fabric and is often abbreviated as "K" in patterns.

Purl: The purl stitch creates a bumpy texture on the fabric and is often abbreviated as "P" in patterns.

Yarn over (YO): This technique adds an extra stitch and creates small eyelets in the fabric.

Increase: There are various methods for increasing stitches, such as yarn overs or knitting into the front and back of a stitch.

Decrease: Similarly, there are different ways to decrease stitches, including knitting two together (K2tog) and slip, slip, knit (SSK).

Bind off (or cast off): This is the process of finishing the edge of the knitted piece and securing the stitches so they don't unravel.

Following these instructions carefully is crucial for achieving the intended design of a knitted item.

Chapter Seven

How to Knit a Messenger Bag Purse

This section will explore knitting a small messenger bag using a circular knitting machine. We will make this pattern in three different sizes: the small size, which is a handbag; the medium size, which is a shoulder bag; and the large size, which is a crossbody bag. In this chapter, we will go through every step of the process.

The bag for this project measures approximately 8 inches wide. The small size measures about 11 inches tall, the medium measures about 18 inches tall, and the large measures about 22 inches tall. The bag is the perfect size to carry a phone, wallet, keys, and other small items.

There are so many ways to customize a bag. You can add a magnetic clasp, line the inside with fabric, add embellishments to the front, use double knitting to create a pattern on the outside, or try adding a pocket to the inside of the bag.

Regarding timing, it takes about one hour and 20 minutes from beginning to end to knit the small size, about 1 hour and 40 minutes to knit the medium size, and about 2 hours to knit the large size bag.

So, project time will vary from person to person. The technique in this section includes casting on and off a knitting machine, seaming the ends of a knitting machine tube, assembling a bag, and seaming pieces together using the mattress stitch. For this project, we will use a 46-needle Addi King Size Express knitting machine, but you can also make this with the Sentro 48-needle machine; your bag will be a touch wider.

We will Knit the bags using Loops and Threads of impeccable yarn in Putty, Aruba Blue, and Sea Green. We use less than one skein per bag for the small and medium sizes, and for the large size, we use a full skein plus about a quarter of a second skein. You'll also need stitch markers, a crochet hook, a darning needle, and a pair of scissors, as well as any solid item about two or three inches in height to help when we seam— a piece of cardboard— and if you'd like to include one, a knitting tag.

Step 1

Knitting the main piece. Begin by casting onto a 46- or 48-needle machine using scrap yarn. Wrap your yarn around the first needle and then weave the yarn back and forth along all the needles until the end of the row. When you reach the first needle again, thread the yarn into the tensioner. If you're using an Addi, hold the yarn in your hand to provide tension; if you're using a Sentro, place the yarn into the middle tensioner. Knit five rows in the scrap yarn.

When you finish five rows, cut a short tail on the scrap yarn and throw it into the middle of the machine. Then, leave a normal-length tail in the main colour yarn and throw it into the middle of the machine right next to the scrap yarn tail. Hold the two tails close and low as you slowly knit the next row. Go slowly at first, making sure it catches all of your stitches. Knit 110 rows in the main colour.

Leave an extra long tail in the main colours when knitting bags to use later when seaming. However, using a new yarn length for seaming is easier for this pattern than for the yarn tail. So, for the project, you can leave a normal-length yarn tail in the main colour.

A quick note about tension: tension can vary from person to person and from yarn to yarn. When you knit the project, your pieces might come out slightly shorter or longer. It is a forgiving project, so if your pieces come out longer or shorter, it's fine— your bag will just be a little taller or shorter. And in related news, if you'd like to knit a taller bag, knit more rows for the main piece. If you'd like to knit a shorter bag, knit fewer rows. Pull the work up inside the machine when your work touches the table.

When you finish 110 rows, switch back to the scrap yarn. Cut a normal-sized tail in the main colour and throw it in the middle of the machine. Then, cut a short tail on the scrap yarn and put it next to the main colour tail. Hold the two tails close together and low as you slowly knit the next row. Knit five rows in the scrap yarn.

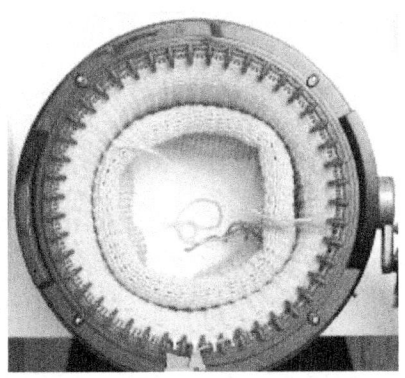

When you finish five rows, cut a short tail on the scrap yarn and continue knitting until the work falls off the needles. Pull the work out of the machine and gently stretch out the stitches. Put the work aside for now while we knit the handle.

Step 2

Knitting the handle. Switch to a 22-needle machine. Cast on like we cast on earlier, wrapping the yarn around the first needle and then weaving the yarn back and forth along all the needles until the end of the row. When you reach the first needle again, thread the yarn into the tensioner. Knit five rows in the scrap yarn. After five rows, please switch to the main colour and knit slowly to ensure it catches all your first few stitches.

For the small handbag, knit 130 rows; for the medium-sized shoulder bag, knit 200 rows; for the large-size crossbody bag, which is the bag we are currently knitting, knit 265 rows. Pull the work inside the machine when your work starts to touch the table. As you continue knitting, especially if you're knitting the large size, you'll need to roll the work as you keep it within the machine. It can get pretty tight at the end because the space inside the machine is so much smaller than the larger machine, but continue rolling the work, and then it'll fall as you knit further, repeat until the end of the project.

When you finish the number of rows needed for your handle, switch back to the scrap yarn. Knit five rows in the scrap yarn. When you finish five rows, cut a short tail in the yarn and continue knitting until the work falls off the needles. Pull the work out of the machine and gently stretch out the stitches. You should now have two finished pieces of knitting: the main piece of the bag and the handle.

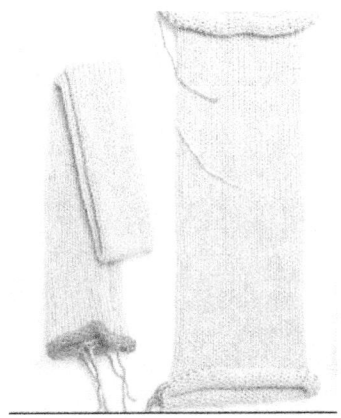

Step 3

Seaming the sides of the tubes. Both pieces have open sides of the tubes. The next step is to use a crochet hook to seam the sides closed. Bring the sides of the tube together, lining up the stitches on each other.

With the two yarn tails to the left side, ensure that when you arrange the stitches, there's one stitch to the right perpendicular to the rest.

Bring your crochet hook under the loop to the right and then pull through the stitch to its left on the top side. Pull through the stitch that's to its left on the bottom side. Continue in that pattern, pulling through the next stitch on the top, followed by the next stitch on the bottom until the end of the row. Pull the yarn tail through when you reach the end of the row; your side is now seamed.

Next, remove the scrap yarn. One side should be removed fairly easily; pull the yarn around and around until it pulls off completely, leaving just the seamed edge. Below is what the final seam will look like.

Next, turn the workaround and use the same process to seam the other side. For the side that's more difficult to remove, identify the top length of yarn running through the stitches and remove the length a few stitches at a time until the end of the row. After that yarn is removed, the rest should be pulled off much more easily.

Next, seam the sides of the handle. Follow the same process as earlier: use a crochet hook to seam both sides of the handle and remove the scrap yarn. Both pieces are now seamed, and the bag is ready to be assembled.

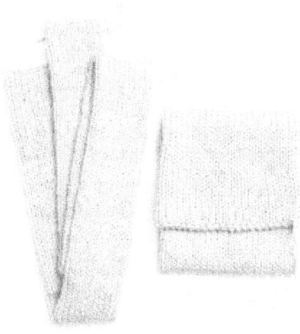

The main piece measures approximately 21 and a half inches long. The handle for the small size measures approximately 16 inches long, the handle for the medium size measures about 40 inches long, and the handle for the large size measures about 48 inches long.

Step 4

Assembling the bag. Lay your main piece vertically, fold the bottom third up, then the top third down.

Line up your handles on the side of the work, then open up the bag again and place any solid item about two to three inches tall in the middle. We will be using a roll of gaff tape, which works well, but you could use many items as long as they're a similar size. Bring the bottom of the bag back up over the item and work to align it evenly with the handles.

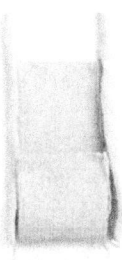

Step 5

Attaching the pieces with stitch markers. Use stitch markers to bring the work together where we'll be seaming. In some projects, you can get away without using the stitch markers even when they're recommended, but in this project, we suggest using them because they will help keep your piece seamed evenly. When you finish the stitch markers in the front, turn the bag around and add them to the corners. Then, turn the back over and add them to the back side, stopping at the same height as the front of the bag. As you use the stitch markers, placing them around the stitches directly under the bars you'll be using for the mattress stitch is helpful. The bottom half of the bag should measure about six inches tall, but the measurement will vary if you're knitting a shorter or longer bag. The bag is ready to seam.

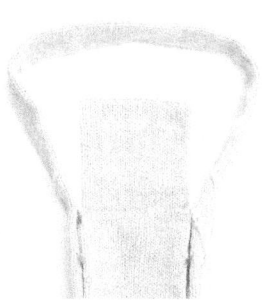

Step 6

Seaming with the mattress stitch. If using the mattress stitch, the first step is identifying two rows of V-shaped stitches on either side of the pieces we'll be joining, going in the same direction. The images below are the rows to bring together the two pieces. Next, look for the bars inside the stitch directly next to the rows.

 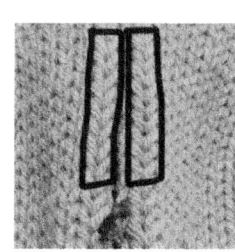 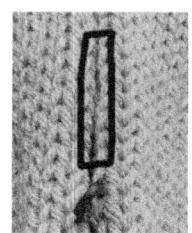

For the pattern, cut a new length of yarn for seaming. To assess how much yarn is needed, casually wrap the yarn around the entire length of what you are seaming, then double the length and usually add a little more to be safe. Then, thread the yarn onto a darning needle and secure it with a knot inside the purse's interior bar. Then, thread it through to the corner of the work.

Look for the bars we discussed earlier. Thread your needle through two bars on the other side of the work. Continue in that pattern, threading through two bars on one side and then two bars on the other until the end of the row.

As you near the stitch markers, remove them as you go. You can also go one stitch at a time if you prefer. Either one stitch at a time or two stitches at a time will work well for the front and back of the bag.

When you reach the corner of the bag, change the process a bit. For the sides, switch to alternating one stitch at a time. For the side with the handle, thread through the two bars of the bottom V-shaped stitch.

For the side of the main bag piece, continue threading through the same interior bars as we did earlier. Continue to the end of the row.

When you reach the corner, turn the work and return to the same mattress stitch style we used to seam the front of the bag.

As you near the end of the seam, make sure to check that you're ending the seam at the same height as the front of the bag. You might need to check that a few times as you work to ensure you're ending the back seam at the same height as the front piece.

When you've got it at the right place, pull through one more loop on the other side to keep the seam closed tightly. Thread the needle to the inside area a few stitches in, secure the yarn tail with a few good knots on an interior bar between the stitches, and then weave in the ends. Next, repeat the same process on the other side of the bag to finish attaching the handle.

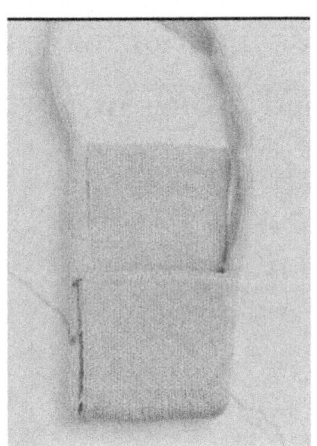

Step 7

Weaving in and trimming the yarn tails. Your work will have lots of yarn tails left out. When working with knitting machine pieces, it's really easy to weave in the ends because there's a center area of the work where you can hide the yarn. Turn your bag inside out, secure all the yarn tails with knots, and then weave in and trim the tails. Turn the work back to the right side.

Step 8

Adding a knitting tag. This step is optional; you can add a knitting tag to the work.

Step 9

Adding a little support. The bags are knitted items, so they have a little stretch. If you'd like to add a little support to the bottom, cut a piece of cardboard about the same size as the bottom and add it to the bag before putting in your items. Or, if you'd like more support, you can sew a fabric lining into the inside of the bag. The small messenger bag is complete.

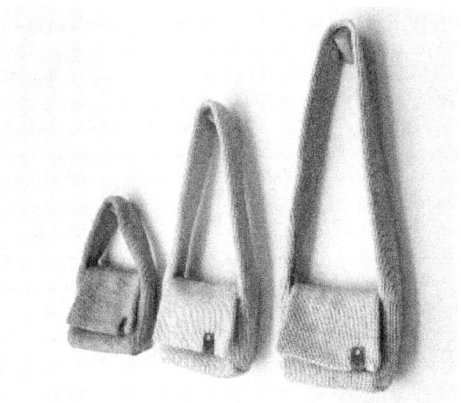

Conclusion

In conclusion, there are many benefits to using circular knitting machines in the textile manufacturing process. These devices lower labor costs and material waste by enabling the quick and efficient manufacture of seamless clothing items like sweaters, caps, and socks. They also offer design flexibility, enabling complex patterns and a range of textures. Additionally, circular knitting machines help to meet the various needs of both consumers and the fashion industry by producing durable and high-quality knitwear. The textile industry can benefit from increased productivity, quality, and innovation using circular knitting machines. Have a swell experience using the circular knitting machine!

Printed in Great Britain
by Amazon

57411067R00056